Blastoff! Readers are carefully developed by literacy experts to build reading stamina and move students toward fluency by combining standards-based content with developmentally appropriate text.

Level 1 provides the most support through repetition of high-frequency words, light text, predictable sentence patterns, and strong visual support.

Level 2 offers early readers a bit more challenge through varied sentences, increased text load, and text-supportive special features.

Level 3 advances early-fluent readers toward fluency through increased text load, less reliance on photos, advancing concepts, longer sentences, and more complex special features.

★ **Blastoff! Universe**

Reading Level

Grade K

Grades 1–3

Grade 4

This edition first published in 2023 by Bellwether Media, Inc.

No part of this publication may be reproduced in whole or in part without written permission of the publisher. For information regarding permission, write to Bellwether Media, Inc., Attention: Permissions Department, 6012 Blue Circle Drive, Minnetonka, MN 55343.

Library of Congress Cataloging-in-Publication Data

LC record for Architect available at: https://lccn.loc.gov/2022005455

Text copyright © 2023 by Bellwether Media, Inc. BLASTOFF! READERS and associated logos are trademarks and/or registered trademarks of Bellwether Media, Inc.

Editor: Betsy Rathburn   Designer: Andrea Schneider

Printed in the United States of America, North Mankato, MN.

Table of Contents

Checking Blueprints	4
What Is an Architect?	6
At Work	10
Becoming an Architect	18
Glossary	22
To Learn More	23
Index	24

Checking Blueprints

blueprints

An architect is planning a new building! She checks her **blueprints**.

She must make sure the building's walls will fit together. Soon, **construction** will begin!

What Is an Architect?

People need places to live and work. People also need places to shop and play.

Architects **design** houses and stores. They also plan outdoor places like bridges and parks.

Golden Gate Bridge

construction area

office

Architects work in offices.
They work in construction areas.

They use math and **physics** to make sure plans work. They make sure projects are safe and beautiful!

Famous Architect

Name — Zaha Hadid

Born — October 31, 1950

Died — March 31, 2016

Birthplace — Baghdad, Iraq

Schooling — American University of Beirut, Architectural Association School of Architecture

Known For — Award-winning architect who designed many famous buildings around the world

At Work

Architects are busy people. They meet with **customers**. They learn what customers want and need.

Then, they use **drafting tools** to make designs. They build **models** of the designs.

drafting tools

pipes

Architects plan the parts of buildings that people can see.

They also plan where wires and pipes will go. They plan carefully so people will be comfortable!

Using STEM

Science — test plans to make sure they work

Technology — use computer programs to draw plans

Engineering — choose strong, safe building materials

Math — measure parts of buildings

Architects make their buildings safe and **accessible**. They make sure everyone can use them!

building made from reused materials

They study their work's **impact**. They make sure buildings are safe for the **environment**.

Architects meet with **engineers** and builders. They help choose building **materials**.

They solve problems. They make sure projects are finished on time!

Architecture in Real Life

safe buildings

strong bridges

beautiful parks

Becoming an Architect

Architects are **creative**. They are good at math and solving problems.

They go to college. They take math and science classes. They work with computers.

After college, architects train. They work with **expert** architects. They learn on the job.

How to Become an Architect

1. go to college

2. train with expert architects

3. pass test to get license

They take a test to get their **license**. Architects make the world safer and more beautiful!

Glossary

accessible—able to be used by people of all abilities

blueprints—plans that show how something will be made

construction—the act of building something

creative—able to make new things or think of new ideas

customers—people who buy goods or services

design—to make a plan for a building, object, or pattern

drafting tools—tools that architects use to create their plans; drafting tools include computer programs, a drawing board, rulers, and special pencils.

engineers—people with science training who design and build machines, systems, or structures

environment—the natural world

expert—having a lot of knowledge or experience in something

impact—the effect of something on another object or the surrounding environment

license—a document that gives architects permission to work

materials—the things used to build something

models—miniature versions of buildings, bridges, and other structures

physics—a science that deals with matter, energy, heat, light, electricity, motion, and sound

To Learn More

AT THE LIBRARY

Borgert-Spaniol, Megan. *Construct a Tiny House!: And More Architecture Challenges*. Minneapolis, Minn.: Abdo Publishing, 2021.

Brody, Walt. *How is a Building Like a Termite Mound?: Structures Imitating Nature*. Minneapolis, Minn.: Lerner Publications, 2022.

Miller, Derek. *The STEM of Skyscrapers*. New York, N.Y.: Cavendish Square, 2021.

ON THE WEB

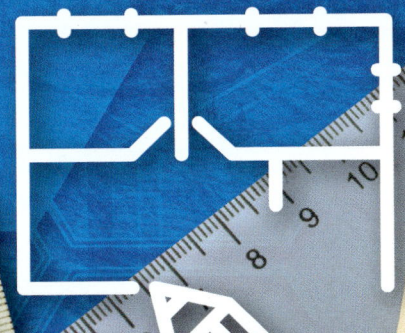

Factsurfer.com gives you a safe, fun way to find more information.

1. Go to www.factsurfer.com.
2. Enter "architect" into the search box and click 🔍.
3. Select your book cover to see a list of related content.

Index

accessible, 14
architecture in real life, 17
blueprints, 4
bridges, 6
builders, 16
building, 4, 5, 12, 14, 15, 16
college, 18, 20
computers, 18
construction, 5, 8
creative, 18
customers, 10
design, 6, 10
drafting tools, 10
engineers, 16
environment, 15
Hadid, Zaha, 9
houses, 6
how to become, 20
impact, 15
license, 21
materials, 15, 16
math, 9, 18

models, 10, 11
offices, 8
parks, 6
physics, 9
pipes, 12, 13
plans, 4, 6, 9, 12, 13
problems, 17, 18
projects, 9, 17
safe, 9, 14, 15, 21
science, 18
stores, 6
train, 20
using STEM, 13
wires, 13

The images in this book are reproduced through the courtesy of: Syda Productions, front cover (architect); S-F, front cover (background); ABCDstock, p. 3; NDAB Creativity, pp. 4-5; Leszek Glasner, p. 5; engel.ac, p. 6 (Golden Gate Bridge); xijian, pp. 6-7; Zero Creatives/ AgeFotostock, pp. 8-9 (construction area); Monkey Business Images, p. 8 (office); drew farrell/ Alamy, p. 9 (Zaha Hadid); Gorodenkoff, pp. 10 (drafting tools), 12-13; ME Image, pp. 10-11; David Papazian, p. 12 (pipes); Huntstock/ Getty Images, p. 14; hollandfoto, pp. 14-15; Rido, pp. 16-17; pinyo bonmark, p. 16 (building materials); Claudio Divizia, p. 17 (safe buildings); Hien Phung Thu, p. 17 (strong bridges); Prisma by Dukas Presseagentur GmbH/ Alamy, p. 17 (beautiful parks); Phynart Studio, p. 18 (inset); PR Image Factory, pp. 18-19; lightfieldstudios, p. 20; Chaay_Tee, pp. 20-21; koosen, p. 23 (hard hat); Garsya, p. 23 (tools).